GYMNASTICS

ILLUSTRATED BY MARY ANN DUGANNE
FRANKLIN WATTS | NEW YORK | LONDON | 1976

GYMNASTICS GYMNASTICS GYMNASTICS GYMNASTICS GYMNASTICS GYMNASTICS

BY ROSS R. OLNEY

GYMNASTICS

◄A FIRST BOOK►

Cover design by Mike Stromberg

Photographs courtesy of: German Information Center: p. 5; Ross D. Olney: p. 39; Swedish Information Service: p. 35; United Press International: pp. 27, 43, 49, 57; United States Gymnastics Federation: pp. 23, 31, 47, 52.

Library of Congress Cataloging in Publication Data

Olney, Ross Robert, 1929–
    Gymnastics.

    (A First book)
    Includes index.
    SUMMARY: Describes gymnastic apparatus and equipment and the events in competition and how they are judged.
    1. Gymnastics — Juvenile literature. [1. Gymnastics] I. Duganne, Mary Ann. II. Title.
GV511.045   796.4'1   75–34478
ISBN 0–531–00849–5

CONTENTS

1

1   IN THE BEGINNING

2

4   APPARATUS

3

14 PERSONAL EQUIPMENT

4

18 JUDGING

5

22 WOMEN'S EVENTS

6

38 MEN'S EVENTS

61   INDEX

1 IN THE BEGINNING

No one knows how or when gymnastics began. Most likely the first gymnast was an early human skilled in swinging from tree branch to tree branch. If this was the beginning, one thing is almost certain, it wasn't long before the tree swingers were challenging each other to find out who was best. Perhaps they wanted to know who could swing the greatest distance, or the highest up, or with the most grace and skill.

Old stone cuttings show that the Egyptians enjoyed building human pyramids and doing balancing stunts as early as 2100 B.C. The Chinese were probably performing such **acrobatics** even before this.

Try to imagine where the pommel horse, also called the side horse, exercises of modern gymnastics began. Why is it even called a horse? The fact is, the early Persians were practicing side horse movements in 500 B.C. as part of training for war. They mounted, dismounted, and swung gracefully around the saddle while racing their horses at high speeds. The names of the parts of today's gymnastic pommel horse (fig. 3, page 10), remind us of the long-ago time when a real animal was used. There is a "neck" (to the left), a "saddle" (in the center), and a "croup" (to the right). Not so long ago pommel horses even had a raised end like a horse's neck and a real tail.

Perhaps no other people in the history of the world so glorified the human body in athletics as the ancient Greeks. The word **gymnastics** comes from them. They developed sports programs and physical education exercises to build the body. The first Olympic Games was held in Greece in 776 B.C.

The Romans too practiced gymnastics. They included tumbling, climbing, swinging, horse and saddle mounting and dismounting exercises in their training for war.

Although nearly forgotten, gymnastics survived through Europe's Dark Ages to become once again popular in the West.

Today, the stunts that began mainly as military training are performed throughout the world for entertainment and pleasure. This book describes some of the most difficult and demanding gymnastic routines performed in international competition. Whether or not you already have an interest in the sport, you get interested fast when you see a double back flip off the rings, or an inverted crucifix, or a double twisting somersault off the high bar. And whether or not you are in training to perform these routines, you are excited by seeing the experts do them.

Most of us owe our interest in gymnastics to television. It has shown us highly skilled athletes performing daring feats. The technology of stop-action and slow-motion camera work helps us better understand the fast-moving routines. Still, at the end of it all, we mostly have a memory of something beautiful, and don't understand why one gymnast won and another lost. The following chapters are a kind of slow-motion camera, except they take you behind the scenes for a look at the basics of the ancient, daring, beautiful sport called gymnastics.

2 APPARATUS

Gymnastics demands strength, endurance, grace, and agility. Years of practice and hard work are necessary before most of the movements described in this book can be accomplished.

Not even the simple, beginning stunts should be attempted without coaching. There are two main reasons. Without good coaching, the gymnast can learn the basics wrong. Valuable time and energy must then be spent relearning them correctly. There is always the chance of injury in this sport. The possibility of getting hurt increases as the stunts get harder to do. Some of the advanced movements can be dangerous to limb and even life.

The younger the gymnast is when training begins, the better. Young bodies are more flexible and more easily trained.

Many elementary and high schools have excellent gymnastics programs. Gymnastics clubs have sprung up across the country as interest in the sport has increased. In 1971, for example, there were only four private gymnastics clubs in Southern California. In 1975, the number had

grown to fifty-eight, and it continues to climb each year. Gymnastics has become one of the most popular sports.

The study of gymnastics begins with simple movements. The somersault and the cartwheel, the front scale and the handstand are some. Gradually the student develops strength and flexibility, and does handsprings and other basic floor exercises.

In international competition, there are different events for men and women. You probably are familiar with them if you have watched gymnastics programs on television. There are six events for men: the **floor exercise,** the **pommel horse,** the **still rings, vaulting,** the **parallel bars,** and the **horizontal bar.** For women in major competitions, there are the **floor exercise, vaulting,** the **balance beam,** and the **uneven parallel bars,** for a total of four events.

Many high schools and colleges include **tumbling** and **trampoline** along with the usual events. These have faded from international competition because they duplicate movements performed in the main events. The trampoline, however, is still used as a training device by all gymnasts.

The men's exercises stress strength and endurance. The women's events have gradually changed to stunts that stress grace, beauty, and balance. The only events that still remain similar for both men and women are the floor exercise and vaulting. But the women's floor exercise has elements of dancing and is done to music while the men's floor exercise is not.

Quality gymnastic equipment will last at least ten years, and some will last fifty years. Rarely will a good parallel bar snap, or a supporting wire give way, though such has happened. Gymnastics is not a sport for the faint-hearted, but equipment breakage is not one of the worries of a performing gymnast.

UNEVEN PARALLEL BARS
(FIG. 1)

Uneven bars are used by women gymnasts only. The upper bar is set at a fixed height of 90⅞₆ inches above the floor. The lower bar is adjusted for each gymnast so that when she is swinging from the upper bar, the lower bar is at the bending point of her hips. The gymnast must swing in a smooth motion around the lower bar at the hips, and not jerk or explode around the bar.

Uneven parallel bars have mats placed beneath and on both sides so that the gymnast can dismount with protection in either direction.

BALANCE BEAM
(FIG. 2)

Many of us would have trouble simply walking the 16-feet, 4⅞-inch length of the balance beam since it is only 4 inches wide. But women gymnasts do difficult and often dangerous routines on the narrow beam. In training, they first work on the floor. They graduate to low training beams, and finally move to the competitive beam, which is set 47¼ inches above the gym floor. At this height, the gymnast can swing her legs without their hitting the floor.

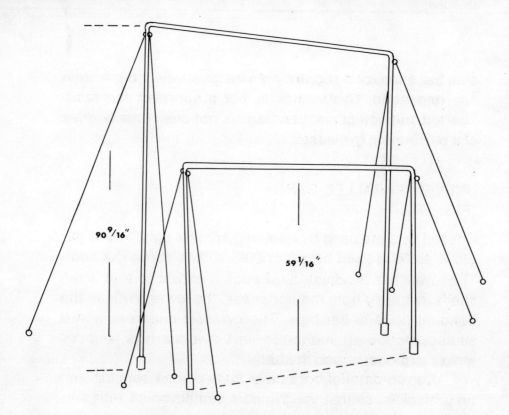

90 9/16"

59 1/16"

FIG. 1 | UNEVEN PARALLEL BARS

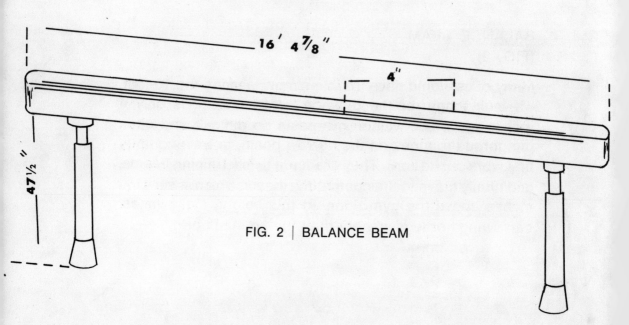

16' 4 7/8"

4"

47 1/2"

FIG. 2 | BALANCE BEAM

The beam is rigidly supported so that there is no movement during the routine. It is surrounded by mats on both sides and at both ends. The end mats can be up to 3 inches thick for safer landings during the dismount part of the gymnast's routine.

POMMEL HORSE AND VAULTING EQUIPMENT (FIG. 3)

The body of the horse is about 64 inches long and supported at from $43\frac{5}{16}$ inches to $45\frac{1}{4}$ inches above the floor on two supporting stands. The body of the horse is padded and covered with leather or vinyl. The horse is set in the middle of a large pad for safety.

The pommels are made of curved wood and extend a height of 5 inches over the body. Although the distance between the pommels can be adjusted, the average width is 17 inches for most gymnasts.

When the pommel horse is to be used for vaulting, the pommels are removed and the height is raised to 53 inches for men (though it remains at $43\frac{5}{16}$ for women vaulters). A 4-inch springboard is placed at one end, and a landing pad up to 6 inches thick is placed at the other end. The springboard is not necessarily there to increase the vaulting height of the vaulter but rather to cushion the feet during the sudden takeoff action. The springboard is placed to the side for women vaulters because they vault over the width rather than the length of the horse.

FIG. 3 | POMMEL HORSE

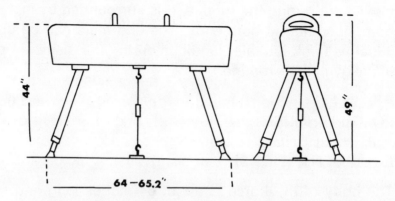

Both men and women compete, though not against each other, in vaulting over the pommel horse. Although basic vaulting techniques are the same, the horse is set at a lower height for women. There is a special pommel horse event performed by men only.

FLOOR EXERCISE MAT

The floor mat is a standard size of 39 feet, 4½ inches per side. It is used by both men and women for floor exercises. Floor exercise rules require the gymnast to use the entire area of the mat. Most floor exercise mats are made 2 feet larger than the regulation surface, and a line on the mat marks off the official competition area. The gymnast may not work outside this line or even touch it.

Some mats are in one piece and can be folded for storage; others can be taken apart for easy storage. The one-piece mats are expensive, costing up to $5000 for a good one.

STILL RINGS (FIG. 4)

Rings are used by men only. They are made of wood and hang from cables attached either to beams in the ceiling of the gymnasium or to a rings frame. Most gymnasts like the rings frame best because it flexes slightly. But most schools have rings attached to the ceiling. The rings must clear the floor by 8 feet, 6 inches, and must have cables which are attached 18 feet, 4 inches above the floor. This means that a gymnast can hang by his hands and not touch the floor with his feet.

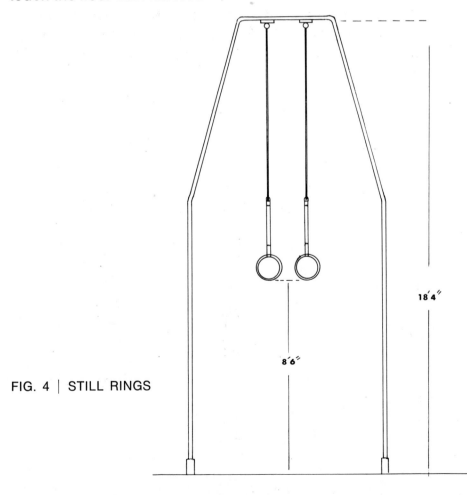

FIG. 4 | STILL RINGS

PARALLEL BARS (FIG. 5)

The rails of this apparatus are made of wood. Each rail is 11 feet, 6 inches long and oval-shaped with an average thickness of about 2 inches.

The rails have a certain amount of flex or springiness. They can be adjusted higher so that a taller gymnast can hang by his upper arms without touching the floor with his feet. They can be moved farther apart or closer together to suit each gymnast.

The rails will generally be around 5 feet, 6 inches off the floor and about 18 inches apart. Mats cover an area 12 feet wide by 16 feet long around the bars. An extra landing mat is placed on each side. Parallel bars are used by men only.

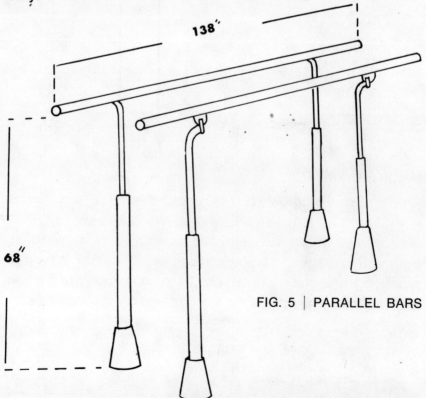

138″

68″

FIG. 5 | PARALLEL BARS

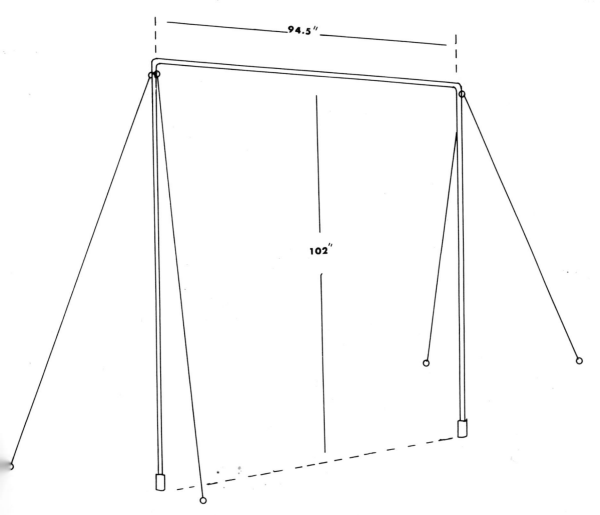

HORIZONTAL BAR (FIG. 6)

Also called a high bar, this is a solid steel bar 94½ inches long and 1⅒ inches in diameter. It can bend up to 3 inches or so under the weight of a swinging male gymnast, then spring back to its straight position. The bar is held in position 102 inches off the floor by posts which are braced with cables. The horizontal bar is used by men only.

3 PERSONAL EQUIPMENT

Men gymnasts generally wear white trousers with tapered legs held up by suspenders. There was a time when no self-respecting gymnast would wear anything but a pure white undershirt top, but no longer. Modern gymnasts wear a competition shirt that fastens under the crotch so it won't pull out during strenuous routines. The shirts can be white or brightly colored. Some have the name of the gymnast's school or club across the chest. Both trousers and shirt are made of a material with good two-way-stretch.

Women gymnasts wear a leotard which is often colorful, with sleeves of a length that suits the individual athlete. Stockings are seldom worn. Women with longer hair usually style it so that it won't fly around during routines.

Chalk is a necessity for all gymnasts. Using it on the hands before an event helps to prevent slipping due to sweat.

Rosin, which is **not** what you see gymnasts rubbing on their hands, is also used. Rosin is used on the soles of the footwear to prevent slipping (especially during balance beam work). It is not applied to the skin.

Gymnastic shoes are generally very lightweight slippers made of a soft material. Some gymnasts wear nothing but socks, or nylon stretch foot stockings normally worn by women under shoes. The advantage of wearing traditional gymnastic slippers with their rubberized, non-slip bottoms is obvious. Plain stockings are lighter in weight and also offer a firm grip on a mat. With most gymnasts, footwear depends on the event.

Handguards made of leather or woven material help to prevent blisters or rips of the skin of the hands. They are used by most advanced gymnasts. Beginners generally do not wear any hand protection, since their routines are more basic and their hands need toughening.

GYMNASTIC SAFETY AND TRAINING EQUIPMENT

When you train in football, you slam into blocking dummies. When you learn fencing, you wear pads and face guards. And when you practice hitting baseballs, they are often thrown by a machine. Gymnastics has its own special training equipment.

Often a coach will "spot" a gymnast in training (fig. 7). This means helping the gymnast not to make a wrong move during a stunt. A helping hand in the small of the back during a back somersault can mean the difference between landing on the feet or landing somewhere else.

FIG. 7 | A COACH SPOTTING A GYMNAST

There are even spotting stools and stands to help a coach reach a gymnast during a difficult or dangerous stunt. Of course spotting is not allowed during competitions.

Nor are safety belts or crash pads, which are even better methods of training gymnasts and protecting them from bad landings. The safety belt supports the gymnast in the air. It allows the gymnast to twist and turn by means of a series of ropes and pulleys attached to the ceiling and controlled by a coach. With a safety belt, the gymnast cannot crash to the floor, even if the stunt fails completely.

Crash pads are very thick, soft landing mats. They are often used long after the gymnast has left the safety belt. They provide a safe landing area if a movement goes wrong.

4 JUDGING

Have you ever wondered how scores at a competition can be so close from so many different judges? Generally they are within a few tenths of a point.

Not long ago wide variations in scores were quite common. Judges were picked because of their general knowledge of the sport, and quite often the first competitor became the standard by which all of the others were judged. Personal opinion played a big part in judging and there were few guidelines to follow.

Now there are strict standards and a set of competitive rules for judging that allow almost no room for error from any judge. Gymnastic scores in every event are based on the Federation of International Gymnastics (F.I.G.) Code of Points. The first such code was written in 1949, and established rules for evaluating the performance of a gymnast. The code has been revised several times since then to keep up with the changing events and emphasis on stunts.

If you want a copy of the code, write to United States

Gymnastics Federation, Box 4699, Tucson, Arizona 85717. You'll gain a much better understanding of how the scores can be so equal after a competitive routine.

Basically, here's how it all works.

Each stunt or specific movement in a gymnastics routine has been given a degree of difficulty. Within certain guidelines, the gymnast can combine these specific movements to create an original arrangement. In international, Olympic, and most collegiate contests, the gymnast then performs his or her routines before judges who are familiar with the F.I.G. Code of Points and method of judging.

With the exception of vaulting, which is judged in a different way, judging for men follows this set of factors.

1.	Difficulty	3.4 points
2.	Combination	2.6 points
3.	Execution	4.0 points
		10.0 points

For women the factors are slightly different.

1.	Difficulty	5.0 points
2.	Originality and composition	2.0 points
3.	Execution	2.0 points
4.	General impression	1.0 points
		10.0 points

Then there are A, B, and C parts in gymnastics.
A. Less or lower difficulty
B. Medium or intermediate difficulty
C. High or superior difficulty

In floor exercise, pommel horse, rings, parallel bars, and horizontal bars (everything but vaulting) the male gymnast's routine must contain at least five A parts, five B parts, and one C part.

The only change from this strict set of requirements is that the gymnast can do a C part in the place of a B part. In other words, he may use a more difficult stunt to replace a less difficult one.

If his routine contains the correct number of stunts in the correct (or better) degrees of **difficulty,** he will be awarded 3.4 points. If not, he will lose percentages of points according to a strict schedule in the F.I.G. Code.

The **combination** part of the set of three factors in male judging covers the way the selection of stunts is arranged to create a routine. Let's take a look at a floor exercise for better understanding. The gymnast will be awarded the full 2.6 points of the total of 10 if his floor exercise lasts between 50 and 70 seconds, if he uses the entire floor space (and does not go outside it), if his exercise forms a harmonious and rhythmical whole, and if it includes stunts of balance, hold, strength, leaps, kips, and tumbling skills such as somersaults.

There are certain things he cannot do such as wrong movements, anything outside the floor area, repeating skills. Points are deducted for mistakes according to a strict penalty point system.

Under the **execution** factor in the set of three, the male gymnast can be awarded 4.0 points for perfection. For each error he makes during his routine, a certain preset penalty point system is in effect.

This set of three factors is the way the men are judged in all but vaulting, and the set of four is the way women are judged in all but vaulting. The women's factors, however, include **originality** and **general impression** in addition to difficulty and execution.

When you see the judges agree on scores of 8.5, 9, 9, 9, and 9.5 for a performance, you know that the gymnast has been very, very good indeed. And you can see that the judges have closely followed the point system. In competition, the high and the low scores are discarded to protect the gymnast further, and only the others are averaged. In the example above, the average would be 9.

The judges are held to strict accounting for deductions. Quite plainly, the judges must be experts on the sport, for some routines go so fast that only an expert can separate the specific parts.

Vaulting is judged separately. Both men's and women's vaulting is rated according to difficulty (the rating assigned to each vault), preflight (from the springboard to the horse), postflight (from the horse to the mat), and form and execution (throughout the vault). Vaults are a one-stunt event. It is the only event where the gymnast who has done poorly can try again. Each vault has a list of deductions such as poor position, touching the horse with anything but the hands, uncertain or heavy landing, which judges use to evaluate the performance.

5 WOMEN'S EVENTS

All gymnastics requires strength and smooth muscle development. But women's events also stress grace and beauty, flexibility and suppleness.

FLOOR EXERCISE

The floor exercise for women is similar to the men's event, but stresses more dancelike movements and is actually done to music. The event is a series of movements based on tumbling exercises. The gymnast picks her own music and develops her own routine within the guidelines of the F.I.G. Code of Points structure.

She walks gracefully to the starting point, hears a brief introduction on the music she has planned, and goes into her routine. She must use the entire mat area, so she works out a routine that uses sides as well as diagonals. She has from 1 minute to 1 minute and 30 seconds to complete her routine.

She must show good balance, coordination, dynamic moves with lightness on landings, grace, beauty, flexibility, and suppleness in all parts of her body. She must show four moves of medium difficulty (B parts) and three moves of superior difficulty (C parts).

There are dozens of different stunts in the women's floor exercise, but almost certainly the gymnast will use both the Back Walkover (fig. 8) and the Front Walkover, which is the same stunt in reverse. These are very popular floor exercise moves of medium difficulty. Note that the legs must be completely split for best execution.

FIG. 8 | FORWARD WALKOVER

The Aerial Walkover (fig. 9) becomes a difficult stunt if the gymnast's shoulders are the lowest point of the walkover, and if the landing is soft and without a bending of the legs.

Soaring higher than the gymnast's head for the best points rating is the graceful Back Layout Somersault (fig.

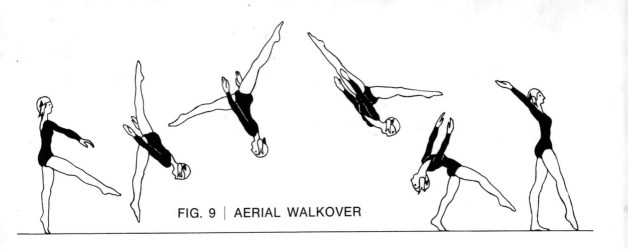

FIG. 9 | AERIAL WALKOVER

10). The body should be straight, or slightly arched, and the legs should be extended. This stunt can be made even more difficult, daring, and complicated by an expert if she adds a full twist, or even turns it into a Double Twisting Back Somersault.

Most of the balance beam movements are also used in floor exercise routines.

FIG. 10 | BACK LAYOUT SOMERSAULT

UNEVEN
PARALLEL BARS

In this event the gymnast attempts to complete her routine without a stop, emphasizing continuous swinging movements. Any stop is considered a rest point and is penalized. Upper arm, shoulder, and upper torso strength is required for uneven parallel bar competition. This strength should not be obvious as the gymnast circles the bars.

The gymnast must show four moves of medium difficulty and three moves of superior difficulty during her routine.

There are many uneven parallel bar movements used in competition. A great variety of releases, regrasps, kips, and twists are all accomplished during the swinging parts. To get on the bars in the first place, the gymnast may use the Glide Kip to a Support Mount (fig. 11).

One of the most exciting moves of all, and with a superior difficulty rating, is the Forward Hip Circle to an Eagle Catch (fig. 12). This one is often seen on television during international meets.

A gymnast might fall from the bars during her routine, but if she can remount and continue, she is permitted to do so with a one-point deduction from her score.

Dismounts from the parallel bars are as exciting and dramatic as the performance itself, and there are a wide variety of them with different degrees of difficulty. Landings from dismounts must be controlled and secure. Any step or hop to help balance after a dismount means a loss of points.

FIG. 11 | GLIDE KIP TO A SUPPORT MOUNT

FIG. 12 | FORWARD HIP CIRCLE
TO AN EAGLE CATCH

BALANCE BEAM

Posture and good body carriage are very important in balance beam routines. Many of the movements performed on the balance beam are like those performed during a floor exercise, but since they are being done on a narrow beam, the difficulty rating goes up. For example, pivots and leaps during a floor exercise might be classed as medium difficult, while the same ones might be rated with a superior difficulty on the balance beam.

The gymnast should keep moving through her routine once it has started. The routine starts when the gymnast touches the beam and ends when her feet touch the mat during dismount. She has from 1 minute and 15 seconds to 1 minute and 35 seconds for her performance. A warning signal is sounded by the judges on all events where time is limited.

Four medium difficult and three superior stunts are required here as in the other events, and also a good balance between dance movements and tumbling movements. The gymnast may mount the beam from any angle.

A very difficult mount with a superior rating is the Forward Walkover, similar to the walkover in the floor exercise moves shown in figure 8. The gymnast gets a running start and walks over onto the beam. There is also a One-Armed Front Walkover and a One-Armed Back Walkover used by skilled gymnasts during a balance beam routine. These have a superior difficulty rating and take years to perfect.

FIG. 13 |
CARTWHEEL

FIG. 14 | STAG LEAP

One of the most recognizable of basic gymnastic moves, made considerably more difficult when attempted on the balance beam, is the Cartwheel (fig. 13). Another is the dramatic Stag Leap (fig. 14), a good balance beam move since the rules require that the entire length of the beam be used during the routine. Good height, a complete split of the legs, and a light-as-a-feather landing are important when making this move.

Dismounts can be made off the side or off the end of the beam.

VAULTING

Vaulting is scored under a different system than the other events, and is the one event where the gymnast tries two times. She can try the same vault twice or two different vaults during her two times up. Also, if she feels her running start is not right, she can stop and try again up to the point where she touches the horse. Her first vault is scored during her brief rest period between vaults, and at that time she can decide whether or not to try the same vault again. Or she might decide to try a different vault to better her score. In any case, the vaulter must tell what she is going to do, and she must accept the score from the second vault if she changes vaults.

Vaults are made off a springboard over the width of a horse with the pommel removed. The vaulter must be strong and quick during her run, explosive during her take-off, and she must get greater height on the postflight than

on the preflight. The hands must be quick and sure, and the landing must be secure, with no balancing hop or step.

The Front Handspring is a popular vault among women gymnasts and if the body is brought to a pike position during the postflight part of the vault, the vault then becomes a Yamashita (fig. 15). This is a stunt as important to women as it is to men vaulters.

Twisting vaults are very popular. From a handspring

FIG. 15 | YAMASHITA

position, the vaulter can twist into a Giant Cartwheel or even half-twist into a handstand and half-twist off. Both of these twisting stunts have a superior difficulty rating.

Women's vaults are judged on four factors: difficulty (a rating assigned to each particular vault by the F.I.G.), preflight phase of the vault (from board to horse), post-flight phase of the vault (from horse to mat), and form and execution throughout the vault.

6 MEN'S EVENTS

Unplanned movements are not made in a gymnastic routine. A last-minute substitution would be out of the question. The gymnast has practiced and practiced his routine until he knows every movement and every possible variation.

There is very little room for experimenting in gymnastics. There is a position for each movement, and that is the correct position. Any deviation from it, whether the gymnast is tall or short, is wrong.

FLOOR EXERCISE

This event probably demands more physical exertion than any of the other men's events. Yet part of the idea of the event is to make very difficult moves look easy. The gymnast must exhibit one movement of superior difficulty, five of medium difficulty, and five of lower difficulty during his routine, for the traditional eleven-part requirement in

men's gymnastics. The exercise must, according to the rules, be harmoniously rhythmical.

The gymnast is given a starting signal from the judge, and he walks to a preselected starting point. This can be anywhere on the mat the gymnast chooses. Usually it will be near one corner, since most gymnasts go through their most difficult C parts first and diagonally.

He must cover the entire area by touching each corner at least once, so many gymnasts work diagonally, then back, then down one side to the third corner, then diagonally again to the fourth corner for the dismount. He cannot leave the mat, or touch the boundary lines, until his routine is finished.

Somersault movements are basic in floor exercises. They are also called **flip-flops,** or they can be referred to by their descriptive name such as a "one and one-half" (fig. 16), "back with a full twist," or "double full twist" (fig. 17). But most gymnasts also use the less complicated Single Front Somersault and the Single Back Somersault as parts of their routine.

Most somersaults with a twist are rated very difficult, and anything with a double somersault is also superior. The idea in all flip-flops is to get as much height as possible. Generally a gymnast will build up his speed and momentum with a series of handsprings and round-offs, then explode into a high somersault at the end.

The judges deduct points from the total of 10 for each example of lack of harmony, rhythm, and flexibility during the routine. Gymnasts must be sharp at every moment of their routine, for the judges are also watching for such

FIG. 16 | ONE AND ONE-HALF

FIG. 17 | DOUBLE FULL TWIST

mistakes as a handstand not held perfectly vertical, kneeling, sitting, or other mistakes of execution, and even undisciplinary and unsporting behavior. In some events the gymnast's coach can stand by, but in no case can the coach give instructions to the performer.

All deductions in floor exercises and in all other gymnastic events for both men and women have a certain, preset value. A woman gymnast can actually fall from a balance beam or from uneven parallel bars, for example, and not completely destroy her chances for victory. The fall from the beam (providing she gets back up and keeps going) will cost her a deduction of 0.5 points, and from the bars 1.0 points. The penalty hurts, especially since the highest possible score is only 10 points. Still, the system allows a gymnast to stay in the running even after a very serious error.

STILL RINGS

Once there were still rings and swinging rings events for both men and women in major competitions, but now only the still rings for men remain. This is a difficult, demanding event, where strength of the upper torso, shoulders, and arms is very important.

It is fairly easy for a gymnast to jump to the rings to begin his routine, but many take advantage of the fact that there is no deduction of points if a coach or helper lifts the gymnast to the rings. This event is called "still" rings, and that means that the judges want to see as little motion of the rings as possible. A stable, unmoving beginning is

important. Serious deductions will occur if the judges see any shaking of the rings or unwanted motions of the body during the routine.

There are two main types of movements on the rings: hold positions and swinging positions. The difficult Iron Cross (photo, p. 43) is a hold position. The Front Giant (fig. 18) is a swinging position. (This same stunt performed

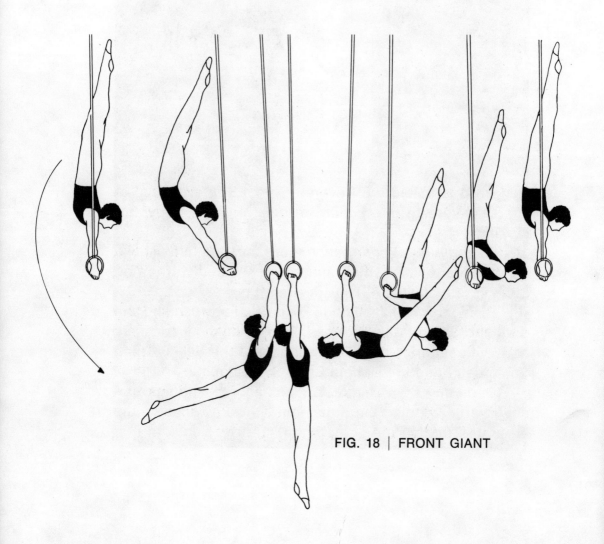

FIG. 18 | FRONT GIANT

FIG. 19 | SHOOT HANDSTAND

backward is called the Reverse Giant.) The swinging, of course, refers to the motion of the gymnast's body, not the rings.

During a still rings routine there must be at least two handstands, one of which must be executed with swing (as in fig. 19) and the other with strength.

Dismounts from still rings are particularly exciting and dramatic, when well performed. Two of the most common, both with superior difficulty ratings, are the Full Twisting Somersault and the Double Back Somersault.

Deductions are made for, among other things, unnecessarily bending the arms, legs, or body, opening the legs, and arching the body too much or not enough.

POMMEL HORSE
(Side Horse)

This is probably the most difficult of all gymnastic skills. Mainly the gymnast swings his legs in circles or scissors while balancing with his hands on the pommels and on the horse itself. Forward and backward circles must be shown (one of these must be shown twice in a row), and the entire area of the horse must be worked, from one end to the other.

Scissors are performed with the legs straddling the horse and swinging back and forth as high as possible in the air. The gymnast's routine must include Front Scissors (fig. 20) and Reverse Scissors, the same movements done in the opposite direction. The legs may not touch the horse or pommels at any time during the routine.

FIG. 20 | FRONT SCISSORS

Smoothness and precise control are critical for good scoring. It would be very difficult for the average spectator to recognize each individual part of a pommel horse routine because the gymnast works so quickly and moves from one part to another so smoothly. The gymnast who moves smoothly and without interruption or pause will generally earn a better score.

The more complicated moves are often variations of circles. For example, the gymnast moves from the pommels to the end of the horse and back again, all the time turning his legs to form circles above the horse.

Pommel horse dismounts include the Front Vault where the gymnast (with or without pike position) arches his body down and alongside the horse. Another is the Piked Loop dismount, where he moves quickly from double leg circles over the end of the horse to a piked dismount.

PARALLEL BARS

In this event there is perhaps more room for error — and also more room to show a variety of movements than in any other event. The bars can be used to show stunts from many other events such as tumbling, side horse, and even some of the strength moves from the still rings.

The gymnast must release the bars, then grasp them again while avoiding a pause in his movements. A pause or a hold of a position of one second is considered to be a stop on the bars — only three stops are allowed. The routine must consist of swing, flight, and hold moves, but

with more swing and flight moves used than holds. One medium difficulty move above or below the bars must be shown where both hands are released. One superior difficulty move must be a swinging stunt.

A gymnast can mount the bars in any one of a number of ways, including running and springing from a board. The Peach Handstand (fig. 21) is a popular mounting movement.

FIG. 21 | PEACH HANDSTAND

Almost never missed during a routine is the Stutz (fig. 22). Depending on the height attained during the turn, the difficulty rating can go very high. If the move is ended in a handstand position held for one second, a superior rating is given.

Dismounts from parallel bars include front somersaults (fig. 23), back somersaults, and combinations of these, such as the very difficult Full Twist Back Somersault and the equally difficult Double Back.

FIG. 22 | STUTZ

FIG. 23 | FRONT SOMERSAULT

HORIZONTAL BAR
(High Bar)

This is another event in which specific moves must be made. The routine must contain only swinging parts and must proceed without pause or interruption. At least one move must be made by the gymnast in which both hands release and regrasp the bar at the same time. At least one move must be made with the gymnast's back to the bar. One movement must be shown in which the gymnast's body spins one full turn on its own axis.

The horizontal bar is generally the last event in a gymnastics meet. It is often the one most cheered by spectators because it often appears to be most spectacular. The very high arches of the skilled gymnast's dismount usually brings especially loud cheers from the onlookers.

Many of the moves are similar to those seen on the parallel bars, and there is great variety.

The most common mount is the Stemme (fig. 24) which follows the quick forward and backward swing allowed just as the gymnast jumps to grasp the bar. The Stemme brings the gymnast into a handstand position, but this, of course, is not held but only passed through on the way to the first swing.

Swings from a handstand position are called Giant Swings. It is a Forward Giant if the swing is to the front, a Reverse Giant if the swing is backward.

For the skill showing the release and regrasp of both hands at the same time, the gymnast might use the Vault (fig. 25).

FIG. 24 | STEMME

FIG. 25 | THE VAULT

During the dismount from the high bar, many gymnasts fling 12 feet into the air on the way to the mat. The dismount can be as daring as the gymnast's skill will allow. Double Somersaults (fig. 26) with or without Twists are very popular.

FIG. 26 | DOUBLE SOMERSAULT

VAULTING

Vaulting, scored differently than the other events, requires one move — or part — from the gymnast. This move is a single vault over the length of a horse (fig. 27), with the pommels removed. Although the approach is not scored, the vaulter may make an approach run of up to 65 feet, 7 inches, before his feet hit the springboard. A good approach, building in speed, assures the vaulter of a good chance for height, which is important in vaulting.

The vaulter should use his hands to push off the horse at some point during his flight off the springboard, but he

FIG. 27 | THE STANDARD VAULT

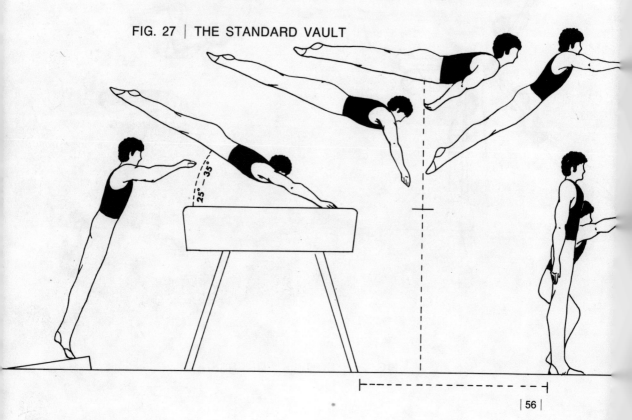

may not touch the horse with any other part of his body. His vault must increase in height from preflight to postflight.

There is a list of specific vaults in the F.I.G. Code, and each vault is given a rating. The vaulter tells the judges which vault he is planning to attempt. At international competitions and some collegiate meets, competitors are generally so skilled that only the highest-rated vaults are selected.

Specifically, the vault must carry the gymnast $\frac{4}{5}$ of the height of the horse *over* the horse during the postflight stage of the vault. The vault must carry the vaulter $1\frac{1}{4}$ the length of the horse *beyond* the horse (if the vault was from the neck, or far end), or 1 length of the horse beyond the horse (if the vault was from the croup, or near end of the horse). Unless the vaulter is into the final stage of international competition, he may choose to take a second vault. If he does, then only the score of the second vault will count.

There are more than a dozen rated vaults, with some of them earning more than 9 points of a possible 10, and one or two earning *10* of 10, if performed perfectly.

The dangerous Cartwheel Back Somersault (fig. 28) has a rating of 10!

The ratings, remember, are not necessarily what the gymnast will earn, but are only what it is possible to earn if the stunt is perfect. Rarely is a perfect score given. But the higher the rating of the vault (or any other stunt), the more minor mistakes the vaulter can make and still get an excellent score. If he is slightly off balance after landing

FIG. 28 | CARTWHEEL
BACK SOMERSAULT

from a Double Somersault, he will be penalized less than the same off-balance from a Single Somersault landing.

But before the young gymnast rushes out to try an extremely difficult stunt just because more small errors can be made without hurting the score, he should remember that there is a deduction judges can make for a competitor's attempting something too difficult for his skills.

So it all balances out.

INDEX

Acrobatics, 1
Aerial Walkover, 24
Arching the body, 45

Back Layout Somersault, 24
Back Walkover, 24
Back with a full twist (somersault), 40
Backward circle (horse), 46
Balance, 6, 24
Balance beam, 6, 7–9, 25, 30–34
    dismounts from, 34
    falls from, 42
    posture on, 30
Behavior, assessed in judging, 42
Blisters, 15
Body, carriage of, 30

California, gymnastics clubs in, 4
Cartwheel, 6, 34, 37
Cartwheel Back Somersault, 58
Chalk, use of, on hands, 14
China, 1
Circles (horse), 46
Clothing, 14–15
Coach, behavior of, during event, 42
Coaching, 4
Collegiate meets, 58

Combination, of gymnast's routine, 20
Competition, 2, 18–21
    judging, 18–21
Composition, of gymnast's routine, 19–21
Control, 26
Coordination, 24
Crash pads, 16–17
Croup (pommel horse), 2

Dance movements, 6, 30
Deductions, in judging, 40–42, 45, 59
    preset value, 42
Diagonals (floor exercise), 22, 40
Difficulty factor, 19–21, 24, 26, 30, 37, 38,
    48, 51
Discipline, 42
Dismounting, 7, 9, 26, 30, 34, 45, 48, 51, 53,
    55
    arches, 53
Double Back Somersault, 45, 51
Double full twist (somersault), 40
Double leg circles, 48
Double somersault, 40, 55
Double Twisting Back Somersault, 25

Eagle Catch, 26
Egypt, 1

Endurance, 4, 6
Equipment, 4–15, 16–17
    breakage of, 6–7
    gymnastic safety and, 16–17
Execution, assessed in judging, 19–21, 37
    mistakes in, 42
Exertion, 38
Experimentation, 38

Falls, 42
Federation of International Gymnastics
    Code of Points, 18–21, 22
Flex, 11, 12
Flexibility, 6, 24, 40
Flip-flops, 40
Floor exercises, 6, 10, 20
    balance beam routines, 25, 30–34
    diagonals, 22, 40
    men's events, 38–42
    for women, 22–25
Floor exercise mat, 10, 22, 40
    regulation surface, 10
    starting point, 40
Footwear, 14–15
Form. assessed in judging, 37
Forward circle (horse), 46
Forward Giant (horizontal bar), 53
Forward Hip Circle, 26
Forward Walkover, 30
Front Giant (ring position), 44
Front Handspring, 36
Front scale, 6
Front Scissors, 46
Front Vault (horse), 48
Front Walkover, 24
Full Twist Back Somersault (parallel
    bars), 51
Full Twisting Somersault, 45

General impression (women's judging),
    19
Giant Cartwheel, 37
Giant Swings (horizontal bar), 53
Grace, 1, 4, 6, 22–24
Greece, 2

Gymnastic programs, 3
Gymnastic shirts, 14
Gymnastic shoes, 14–15
Gymnastics
    beginning of, 1–3
    clothing for, 14–15
    equipment breakage, 6–7
    equipment for, 4–15, 16–17
    importance of coaching in, 4
    judging of, 18–21
    popularity of, 6
    safety, 15–17
    sporting behavior, 42
    unplanned movements, 38

Hairstyles, for women gymnasts, 14
Handguards, 15
Handspring, 6, 40
Handspring position, 36–37
Handstand, 6, 37, 45, 53
Harmony, assessed in judging, 40
Height, and difficulty of exercises, 34,
    51
High bar, 13, 53–55
Hold position (rings), 44
Hop, 36
Horizontal bar, 6, 13, 20, 53–55
    dismounts from, 55
    similarity to parallel bar, 53
    swinging parts, 53
Horse, 1, 2, 9–10, 34–37, 46–48
    beginnings of, 1–2
    construction of, 9
    leg movement, 46
    precision, 48

Injury, 4
Inverted crucifix, 2
Iron Cross, 44

Judges, 18
Judging, 18–21, 24, 37, 40–42, 48, 56–59
    A, B, C parts of, 19–20, 24
    factors in, 19–21
    standards of, 18

Kips, 20, 26
Kneeling, 42

Landing pad, 9
Landings, 26, 34, 36
Leaps, 20, 30, 34
Leotards, 14
Low training beam, 7

Mats, 7, 9, 10, 12, 22, 30, 40
Meets, 53
Men's events, 6, 10, 12, 13, 14, 19, 20,
    38–59
    floor exercises, 38–42
    horizontal bar, 53–55
    parallel bars, 48–51
    pommel horse, 46–48
    still rings, 42–45
    vaulting, 56–59
Military training, 2
Momentum, 40
Mounting, of parallel bars, 50
Muscle development, 22
Music, for women's floor exercise, 22

Neck (pommel horse), 2, 6

Olympic Games, 2
One and one-half (somersault), 40
One-Armed Back Walkover, 30
One-Armed Front Walkover, 30
Originality, assessed in judging, 19–21

Parallel bars, 6, 12, 20, 48–51, 53
    mounting, 50
    rails of, 12
    room for error, 48
    stops, 48
Peach Handstand, 50
Penalty point system, 20, 26, 40–42
Perfect score, 58
Persia, 1
Perspiration, 14
Physical exertion, 38

Pike position, 36, 48
Piked Loop dismount (horse), 48
Pivots, 30
Points, in judging, 18–21
Pommel horse, 1, 2, 9–10, 20, 34–37, 46–
    48
Postflight (vaulting), 21, 34, 36, 37, 58
Posture, 30
Practice, 38
Precision, 48
Preflight (vaulting), 21, 34, 36, 37, 58
Pulleys, 16

Ratings, 58
Regrasps, 26
Releases, 26
Remounting, 26
Rest period, 34
Reverse Giant (horizontal bar), 53
Reverse Giant (ring position), 45
Reverse Scissors, 46
Rhythm, 40
Rings frame, 11
Rome, Ancient, 2
Ropes, 16
Rosin, 14–15
Round-offs, 40
Running start, 30, 34

Saddle (pommel horse), 2
Safety, 15–17
Safety belts, 16–17
School gymnastics programs, 4–6
Scissors (horse), 46
Scores, 18–21, 26
Side horse, 1, 2, 9–10
Single Back Somersault, 40
Single Front Somersault, 40
Sitting, mistake in floor exercise, 42
Skill, 1, 4
Skin, of hands, protection for, 15
Slippers, 15
Slow-motion photography, 2–3
Smoothness, 48
Socks, 15

Somersault, 6, 15, 20, 40, 51, 58–59
    Back Layout, 24–25
    back with a full twist, 40
    Cartwheel Back, 58
    double, 40, 55
    Double Back, 45–51
    double full twist, 40
    Double Twisting Back, 25
    Full Twist Back, 51
    Full Twisting, 45
    one and one-half, 40
    Single Back, 40
    Single Front, 40
Speed, 40
Splits, 24, 34
Spotting, by coach, 15–16
Spotting stools, 16
Springboard, 9, 34
Stag Leap, 34
Starting point, 40
Starting signal, 40
Stemme (horizontal bar), 53
Still rings, 6, 11, 20, 42–45
    dismounts from, 45
    hold position, 44
    for men's use only, 11
    reducing motion, 42–44
    shoulder strength, 42
    swinging position, 44
Stockings, 14, 15
Straddling (horse), 46
Strength, 4, 6, 26, 42, 45
Stunts, 20
Stutz (parallel bars), 51
Substitutions, of movements in routine, 38
Support mount, 26
Suspenders, 14

Swinging position (rings), 44
Swinging rings, 42

Takeoff, 34
Television, events on, 2–3, 6
Time limits, 30
Training, 4, 6
Trampoline, 6
Tumbling, 6, 20, 22, 30, 48
Twisting vaults, 36–37
Twists, 26, 55

Uneven parallel bars, 6, 7, 26
    dismounts from, 26
    height of, 7
    importance of smooth motion, 7
    swinging movement, 26
U.S. Gymnastics Federation, 19

Vaulting, 6, 9–10, 19, 21, 34–37, 56–59
    approaches, 56
    height in, 56
    judging of, 21
    scoring of, 34, 37, 56–58
    second chance, 58
    twists, 36–37
    use of hands, 56–58
Vertical, 42

Walkovers, 24, 30
Women's events, 6, 7, 9, 10, 19, 21, 22–37
    balance beam, 30–34
    grace of, 6, 22, 24
    music used in, 22
    uneven parallel bars, 26
    vaulting, 34–37

Yamashita (vault), 36

ABOUT THE AUTHOR

Ross R. Olney is a man of many and varied interests. He is a skin diver, a professional photographer, a hang glider, a skilled camper, a magazine writer, and the author of more than seventy books. A native of Ohio, he now lives with his wife and three sons in Canoga Park, California.